The Coming Rise *of* Christian Education

HOW POLITICAL AND RELIGIOUS TRENDS ARE FUELING A SURGE IN CHRISTIAN SCHOOLING

Stephen R. Turley, Ph.D.

TURLEY TALKS

A New Conservative Age is Rising

www.TurleyTalks.com

Table of Contents

Introduction

Christian education is frustrating. It's frustrating for administrators who struggle to keep their school doors open in the face of limited resources and finances. It's frustrating for teachers who wear a number of different hats all the while maintaining classrooms with minimal support. And it's frustrating for parents and students who lament the scarcity of sports and dearth of elective opportunities that are all too often characteristic of classical schools, let alone the parental stress involved in homeschooling.

I know this frustration well. As a Christian educator for over 16 years, I've often found myself despondent, overwhelmed with the inadequacies of start-up schools and the student attrition that so often accompanies it. It's easy to feel a certain futility in the midst of our efforts to recover a Christian tradition responsible for civilizational splendors without equal, which has nevertheless laid dormant for so long.

And yet, something is happening. This Christian educational tradition is currently experiencing an unprecedented reawakening throughout the Western world. In ways unimaginable just a few years ago, Christian education is experiencing nothing short of a renaissance, of which we are at the very beginnings. However, I'm very concerned that Christian school leaders and teachers remain largely unaware of what is coming their way in the next several years. In the midst of all of our lesson planning, faculty and board meetings, budgeting and conferences, we may be overlooking the rising tsunami of students beginning to form over the horizon. This book seeks not only to dispel any pessimism that may be fueling our current frustration; it's about *preparing* for the abundance that lies ahead; it is about laying the groundwork for your school to go beyond *surviving* and begin *thriving*.

I want to show you why the future of Christian education is incredibly bright, and that your teaching and administrative efforts *will* pay off in ways you may have thought impossible. In order to surmise what to expect in the coming decades, we will explore three interrelated trends that are combining to forge an astonishingly fruitful future for Christian educational endeavors. In our first chapter, we will look at how our world is currently going through an extraordinary religious nationalist renewal. In chapter two, we will discover that the revitalization of the natural family is at the heart of that renewal. In the remaining chapters, we'll find how this revitalized natural family is fueling the rise of Christian education. Chapter three looks at the rise of classical Christian education in the United States. Chapter four explores the Christianization of the educational system in Hungary. Chapter five introduces us to the homeschooling and Christian reforms currently going on in the Russian Federation. Finally, in chapter six, we'll see how the Republic of Georgia has implemented an Orthodox Christian curriculum throughout their public schools.

Together, these trends are indicating an extraordinary future for Christian education, one that can turn your school's posture of surviving into one of thriving. It is my hope that by discovering these trends, parents, administrators, and educators will be encouraged that their efforts in the present are but a foretaste of an even more glorious education renewal yet to come.

CHAPTER ONE

The Religious Nationalist Renewal

According to the World Values Survey, four out of five people in the world, that's 80 percent of the world's population, ascribe allegiance to one of the major historic world religions. In sub-Sahara Africa, Christianity is actually growing faster than the continent's population growth, suggesting massive conversion rates. In the Middle East, more Muslims are attending mosque than ever before in the history of Islam. China is currently experiencing what may be the single greatest Christian revival ever recorded in the history of the church. Hungary's government has declared its commitment to the revitalization of Christian civilization, while Poland has formally declared Jesus Christ as Lord and King over their nation. India is currently experiencing a massive Hindu nationalist revival led by the Bharatiya Janata Party, which is the single largest democratic party on the planet. In the Russian Federation, the Orthodox Church has risen to a prominence not seen since the days of the Tsars. And in

Latin America, Pentecostalism is sweeping throughout the region while more Catholics are attending Mass than ever before. It's no wonder that a number of scholars believe that we are currently experiencing the single greatest religious surge the world has ever seen.[1]

But why? Why is religion surging throughout the world? The answer appears to be intimately bound up with what scholars call *globalism* or *globalization*, a vast interlocking mechanism of technology and telecommunications that creates a single worldwide economic and political system.[2] We all intuitively know what globalism is: Coke-a-cola, McDonald's, Amazon, the International Monetary Fund. Have you ever noticed that all airline pilots sound the same? We're all living today with the same fast-food chains, the same internet search engines, the same computer processors. This is globalization: a one-size-fits-all political and economic system that basically turns the entire world into a giant version of Orlando, Florida!

But globalism has a number of unfortunate consequences, particularly for the frames of reference necessary for a sense of national identity. Because globalization eclipses the nation-state with wider transnational economic and political processes, many scholars believe that globalization is bringing an end to the whole concept of distinct nations. Such a dire prospect is not lost on populations, as it is most

---

[1] Cf. Rodney Stark, *The Triumph of Faith: Why the World is More Religious than Ever* (Wilmington, DE: ISI Books, 2015).
[2] See, for example, Anthony Giddens, *Runaway World: How Globalization is Reshaping our Lives* (New York: Routledge, 2000).

explicitly exemplified in mass unfettered immigration. As Paul Harris has observed, the porous borders which serve to expedite flows of goods within a globalized economy entail a significant increase in levels of immigration, both legal and illegal.[3] This immigration flow trends along the direction of economic activity: Turks flow into Germany, Albanians ebb into Greece, North Africans into France, Pakistanis into England, and Mexicans into the U.S.[4]

Increasingly, the world feels like it is flattening, with one nation in effect blending into the other. As such, the cultural uniqueness so indispensable to the perpetuation of national identities appears to be withering worldwide, with a globalist, monolithic, consumer-based culture taking over. Globalism has thus provoked a worldwide backlash, where populations are turning more and more toward their own culture, customs, traditions, *most especially their religious traditions*, as mechanisms of resistance against what they perceive as the anti-cultural processes of globalization and its secular aristocracy.

This return to a population's culture and religious customs is a process that scholars refer to as *retraditionalization,* a renewed interest in "traditions of wisdom that have proved their validity through the test of history," or "a longing for

[3] Paul A. Harris, "Immigration, Globalization and National Security: An Emerging Challenge to the Modern Administrative State," http://unpan1.un.org/intradoc/groups/public/documents/aspa/unpan 006351.pdf.
[4] Victor Davis Hanson, "The Global Immigration Problem," http://www.realclearpolitics.com/articles/2007/05/the_global_immigra tion_problem.html.

spiritual traditions and practices that have stood the test of time, and therefore can be valued as authentic resources for spiritual renewal."[5] It's important to note that retradition-alization is not limited simply to spiritual renewal or religious revival; it often involves a reconfiguration of political, cultural, and educational norms around pre-modern religious beliefs and practices as a response to the secularizing processes of globalization.[6]

What a number of scholars are recognizing is that one of the major institutions that are being affected by this process of retraditionalization is the family. One study, in particular, found that retraditionalization largely explained the rise of fertility among ethnic enclaves in the nation of Kyrgyzstan, where the researchers found that when minorities felt threatened by the cultural pressures of the wider ethnic majority, the more they turned to procreation and fertility as the primary means of resisting such pressures.[7] However, as we shall discover in the next chapter, within secular globalist societies, retraditionalized families will not remain as enclaves for very long.

---

[5] Leif Gunnar Engedal, "*Homo Viator*. The Search for Identity and Authentic Spirituality in a Post-modern Context," in Kirsi Tirri (ed.) *Religion, Spirituality and Identity* (Bern: Peter Lang, 2006), 45-64, 58.
[6] Ivan Varga, "Detraditionalization and Retraditionalization," in Mark Juergensmeyer and Wade Clark Roof (eds.), *Encyclopedia of Global Religion* (Los Angeles: Sage Publications, 2012), 295-98, 297.
[7] Michele E. Commercio, "The Politics and Economics of 'Retraditionalization' in Kyrgyzstan and Tajikistan," *Post-Soviet Affairs* 31 no. 6 (2015): 529-56.

CHAPTER TWO

The Revitalized Family

At the heart of this religious resurgence is nothing less than the revitalization of the natural family.[8] Scholars such as Eric Kaufmann of the University of London are recognizing that we are in the early stages of a demographic revolution, a revolution where conservative religionists are on course, and these are his words, "to take over the world."[9] What scholars are noticing is that there is a dramatic demographic difference between secularists and conservative religionists. For example, in the U.S., conservative evangelical women have a 30 percent fertility advantage over their secular counterparts, and this demographic deficit has dramatic effects over time. In a population evenly divided

---

[8] The 'natural family' is a term used by the International Organization for the Family to denote a family comprised of father, mother, and children which functions as the natural and fundamental group unit of society. See https://www.profam.org/article-16/the-family-and-development/.

[9] Eric Kaufmann, *Shall the Religious Inherit the Earth? Demography and Politics in the Twenty-First Century* (London: Profile Books, 2010).

between conservatives and secularists, a 30 percent fertility differential means that in one generation, that 50/50 split will turn into a 60/40 split; in two generations, that would widen into a 75/25 split, and in the course of 200 years, it would be a 99 to 1 split.

The Amish and Mormons provide contemporary illustrations of the compound effect of endogamous growth. The Amish double in population every twenty years, and projections have the Amish numbering over a million in the U.S. and Canada in just a few decades; in fact, by the end of next century, the Amish are projected to reach a population of over 300 million! Since 1830, Mormon growth has averaged 40 percent per decade, which means that by 2080, there may be as many as 267 million Mormons in the world, making them anywhere from 1 to 6 percent of the world's population by 2100.

In contrast to the flourishing fertility among conservative Christian families, Kaufmann's data projects that secularists, who consistently exemplify a low fertility rate of around 1.5 (significantly below the replacement level of 2.1), will begin a steady decline after 2030 to a mere 14 to 15 percent of the American population. Kaufmann thus appears to have identified what he calls "the soft underbelly of secularism," namely demography.[10] This is because secular liberalism entails its own "demographic contradiction," the affirmation of the sovereign individual devoid of the restraints of classical

---

[10] Kaufmann, *Shall the Religious*, xv.

moral structures necessitates the freedom not to reproduce. The link between sex and procreation having been broken, modernist reproduction translates into mere personal preference. It thus turns out that radical individualism, so celebrated and revered by contemporary secular propagand- ists, is, in fact, the agent by which their ideology implodes.

In Europe, immigration is ironically making the continent more religiously conservative, not less; in fact, London and Paris are some of the most religiously dense areas within their respective populations. In Britain, for example, Ultra- Orthodox or Haredi Jews constitute only 17 percent of the Jewish population but account for 75 percent of Jewish births. And in Israel, Haredi schoolchildren have gone from comprising a few percent to nearly a third of all Jewish pupils in a matter of five decades and are poised to represent the majority of the Jewish population by 2050. Since 1970, charismatic Christians in Europe have expanded steadily at a rate of 4 percent per year, in step with Muslim growth. Currently, Laestadian Lutherans in Finland and Holland's Orthodox Calvinists have a fertility advantage over their wider secular populations of 4:1 and 2:1 respectively.

Some may think that mass conversions can compensate for this demographic deficit, enticing the children of religious conservatives to break away and join the ranks of the secular. However, this is highly unlikely. The more conservative and vibrant the religious commitment, the more incentives there are for the next generations to remain faithful and concomitantly strong disincentives to leave. Indeed, we have statistics that demonstrate that children growing up in conservative religionist households are highly likely to maintain such conservative religious sentiments into their adult years. We also have studies that show that liberal religionists are more likely to become conservative than the other way around.[11] Thus, with clearly delineated social boundaries and identity markers, conservative endogamous groups are generally very difficult to break up. And Kaufmann's data suggests that the more conservative the group, the greater the demographic discrepancy as compared with secularist procreation.

Demographer Phillip Longman has come to the same conclusion as Kaufmann and others. In a recently published article on the rising birthrates among conservatives in Europe and the United States, Longman notes that liberal critics of the traditional family are actually plagued by a rather inconvenient fact–the feminist and countercultural movements of the 1960s and 70s have not and are not leaving any genetic legacy. While only 11 percent of baby boomer women had four or more children, they made up over 25 percent of the total children born to baby boomers. Conversely, the 20 percent of women who had only one child accounted for a mere 7 percent of the total children born to baby boomers. Specifically, he cites statistics from France, where only about 30 percent of women have three

---

[11] Stark, *Triumph,* 188, 191, 194.

or more children, but they're responsible for over 50 percent of all French births.

Thus, Longman concludes that this fertility discrepancy is "leading to the emergence of a new society whose members will disproportionately be descended from parents who rejected the social tendencies that once made childlessness and small families the norm. These values include adherence to traditional, patriarchal religion, and a strong identification with one's own folk or nation."[12]

Longman notes that this demographic dynamic helps explain, for example, what he calls the gradual shift of American culture away from secular individualism and towards what he calls "religious fundamentalism," or what I would prefer, religious traditionalism. He notes that among states that voted for President George W. Bush in 2004, the fertility rates in those states were 12 percent higher than in states that voted for Sen. John Kerry. Turning his attention across the pond, Longman notes that this demographic discrepancy may account, at least partially, for why Europeans are beginning more and more to reject what he calls the crown jewel of secular liberalism, the European Union. And this is because, as it turns out, those Europeans, who are most likely to identify themselves as "world citizens" and globalists, are also those least likely to have children. Longman cites demographic data that found that those with globalist values, those who had a high

---

[12] https://foreignpolicy.com/2009/10/20/the-return-of-patriarchy/.

enthusiasm for alternative lifestyles and a marked complacency towards cultural traditions and customs, were far less likely to get married and have kids than those who exemplified more nationalist sentiments, such as a deep reverence for nation, culture, custom, and tradition. And so, in Europe and the States, we're finding that the number of children different people have, and under what circumstances, actually correlates very strongly with their beliefs on a wide range of political and cultural attitudes.

We may be seeing a further indicator of this demographic revolution. According to a recent Gallup poll that asked, "What do you think is the ideal number of children for a family to have?" More Americans than at any point since the early 1970s said they considered three or more children as the ideal size of the family.[13] According to the poll, 41 percent said they wanted three or more children, which is up from 34 percent back in 2011. Moreover, the same poll found that those who believed that 4 or more children to be ideal also increased from 9 percent in 2007 to 15 percent in 2018. Gallup has been tracking this question each year for the last several decades, and they found that between the years of 1967 and 1971, attitudes towards the family have changed dramatically. The percentage that wanted a large family fell from 70 percent down to around 50 percent, a 20-point drop, corresponding to the height of the widespread fear concerning overpopulation in the late 1960s and early

---

[13] https://www.cnsnews.com/news/article/natalia-mittelstadt/poll-41-say-families-3-or-more-children-ideal-34-2011.

1970s. Such sentiments fell to an all-time low in 1986, when only 26 percent of those polled wanted a big family.

But there's little question that the last several years have seen a noticeable trend towards a renewed popularity for relatively big families, consisting of 3 or more children. And what's particularly interesting here is that the current average ideal is around 2.7 children per couple, up from 2.5 in 2007 and then again in 2011. Note how this corresponds with Kaufmann's statistic regarding conservative Christian populations in the U.S., who are averaging 2.5 children per couple, which is significantly above the 2.1 replacement threshold. So, the Gallup poll is averaging out at around the same size of the average conservative family found in Kaufmann's studies. We may thus be seeing the beginnings of the transition from a secular globalist conception of the family with very low birth rates to a conservative traditionalist conception of the family with its comparably high birth rates.

But what does this mean for the future of Christian education? Recently, I was talking with a good friend who, over the last several years, has entered the grandfather season of life. He is the father of seven, all grown and married. To date, my friend has 23 grandchildren, with another one on the way. His tribe has increased threefold, and all of his grandchildren are or will be attending classical schools. My friend's situation is not exceptional; the current generation of classical students, along with new families and schools coming into the classical fold, promise to increase the student population significantly over the next decades. If 3 to 4 million children are currently participating in Christian education, we can easily be looking at over 10 million in the next 20 to 30 years. Indeed, a trend is already appearing that indicates extraordinary growth. In what follows, we will look at the developments that have already occurred that collectively suggest a future for Christian education that is grander than anything we could have imagined a decade ago.

CHAPTER THREE

The Renaissance of
Classical Education

Because the renewed natural family is a response to secular globalism, they're rather suspicious of secularized public education. And so, it's no coincidence that this spike in Christian fertility over the last few decades has been accompanied by a massive spike in Christian education, particularly in the United States. Just take the homeschooling phenomenon as an example: In 2003, there were an estimated 2,100,000 children homeschooled nationwide, which grew to 2,500,000 in 2009, representing an average growth rate of 7-15% per year. According to the National Center of Educational Statistics, the percentage of all school-aged children homeschooled in the U.S. increased from 1.7% in 1999 to 3% in 2009, representing a 74% increase over a ten-year period. Today, estimates are anywhere from 3 to 4 percent of American's children are homeschooled, which is 2 to 3 million kids.

However, there is another indicator that retraditionalization is shaping a renewed interest in Christian education, and that is the renaissance of classical education. If you're not familiar with this renewal, classical education dominated Western Civilization for 2,500 years, beginning with the ancient Greeks and developed through the Roman and Christian periods, becoming the foundation for the medieval university. What we know today as a liberal arts education, with its focus on the great works of literature, art, and music, together with the classical languages of Latin and Greek, and the sciences of math and geometry and astronomy, with Christian theology at its center, provided the paradigm of an educated person up until the beginning of the twentieth century. Having been eclipsed by modern secularized educational approaches for decades, classical education is making an astonishingly successful return.

According to the Association of Classical Christian Schools' membership statistics, there were 10 classical schools in the nation in 1994; today, there are over 230. Since 2002, student enrollment in classical schools has more than doubled from 17,000 nationwide to over 41,000. And these are just ACCS affiliated schools. There are estimates that classical Christian schools now number upwards of over 500 in the nation.

Classical homeschool organizations such as Classical Conversations have also thrived, with a current student enrollment of over 60,000. And again, there are estimates that the number of home-school children who receive a classical education may be ten times larger than their conventional peers.

We're also seeing among Catholic schools a mass shift towards rediscovering anew the ancient or traditional way of approaching education. A recent example involves an entire diocese of schools in Michigan who have rejected Common Core by returning to a distinctively Catholic liberal arts education. Moreover, we're seeing the development of networks and organizations such as the Institute for Catholic Liberal Education, and annual conferences that are providing the professional development necessary for a vibrant faculty and administration.

The charter school movement as well, now representing 10 percent of publicly funded schools, is becoming fertile ground for classical education. The Great Hearts Academies operates currently 25 public charter schools in Arizona and Texas, which together enroll 13,000 students with another 13,000 on waiting lists.[14] The Barney Initiative of Hillsdale College has the second-largest network of public classical schools, serving over 6,000 students spanning seven states. Altogether, the total number of classical charter schools may be upwards of 150 in the nation.

---

[14] John J. Miller, "Back to Basics," *National Review* Vol. 67 Issue 19 (October 2015): 42-44.

And we are already seeing the effects of this kind of education. As of 2015, classically educated students had the highest SAT scores in each of the three categories of Reading, Math, and Writing among all independent, religious, and public schools. In fact, even the SAT and ACT are being rivaled by the advent of the CLT or the Classical Learning Test, an evaluation far more reflective of a classical and Christian education than what is represented by contemporary standardized testing. This represents, I think, the beginning of a real transformation in education assessment that has profound implications for what we consider to be an educated person in an increasingly post-secular world. The CLT resembles other standardized tests, but it breaks the area of verbal reasoning down into four sub-areas: philosophy/religion, natural science, literature, and historical/founding documents. Though only a couple of years old, over 90 colleges have agreed to accept the scores for the CLT instead of the SAT and the ACT, and more than 300 high schools across the country are serving as centers for CLT testing.

But the renewal of classical education in the United States is but one indicator of the flourishing future for Christian education. To get a sense of the global nature of this trend, we will discover the educational reforms currently going in Europe as well.

CHAPTER FOUR

Raising a Godly Generation: The Hungarian Vision for Christian Schools

S hortly after his massive landslide win in April of 2018, a victory that gave him his third-straight term as prime minister, Viktor Orban announced his vision to build Hungary into what he called a 'Christian democracy.' Among the distinctive features of a Christian democracy, Orban has focused on a renewed cooperation between church and state in the preservation of their national customs, cultures, and traditions; the protection of the nations' borders so as to protect Hungary's unique values; a diverse application of economic nationalism as an extension of national identity; and a renewed commitment to fostering and furthering the natural family for a flourishing future.[15] But amidst these grand social goals, it's the reforms in Hungary's K-12 education system that just may have the most significant impact for the coming Christian majority.

János Lázár, a very influential Hungarian politician and member of Viktor Orban's cabinet, recently remarked that the single most important institutions of education in Hungary are the Christian parochial schools, and he went on to say that the primary goal of education in Hungary is officially now to raise good Christians and good Hungarians. In fact, he made the argument that "the lesson of the last 1,000 years is that the nation can endure only through religious educational institutions."[16]

As part of that vision, Hungary is transferring many of its public schools over to the Christian church.[17] As a result, the number of Christian parochial schools has been growing quite rapidly, especially since Viktor Orban successfully nationalized the schools that were formerly run by local municipalities. Just to give you an idea of the surge in Christian education in Hungary: In 2010, there were a total of 572 church-operated schools; today, that number has more than doubled to over 1,300! Note that the number of

---

[15] For a development of Orban's vision of a Christian democracy, see my *The New Nationalism: How the Populist Right is Defeating Globalism and Awakening a New Political Order* (Newark, DE: Turley Talks Publishing), 2018.
[16] http://hungarianspectrum.org/2017/09/01/the-orban-governments-penchant-for-religious-educational-institutions/.
[17] http://www.tfp.org/hungary-hands-over-public-schools-to-religious-institutions-2/.

church-operated schools has doubled in just a matter of eight years. In 2010, there were just over 112,000 students attending parochial schools; today, their number has reached nearly 210,000. There are even some communities in Hungary that *only* have Christian schools; in other words, the parochial school is their only school of choice. This trend of only church-run schools, particularly in small towns and villages, has been going on for some time now. Between 2001 and 2011, those attending church-run schools in towns and villages increased by 60 percent, and after Viktor Orban and his Fidesz Party's win in 2010, that number increased again from 2011 and 2014 by an additional 47 percent.[18] According to a recent study, there are nearly 100 villages and 30 larger towns without a single secular public school.[19] The secular public school is fast becoming the minority form of education in Hungary.

By all accounts, these Christian schools are far and away better than secular public schools. Beyond just the moral teachings and the strong sense of sacred nationalism that's taught in most parochial schools, they also receive far more money than do public schools, often times twice the money. In recent years, parochial schools get three times the funding per student than standard public schools. In addition, because they are run by churches and not directly by the state, they can choose their own textbooks and

[18] https://budapestbeacon.com/church-schools-taking-over-in-hungarys-poorer-regions/.
[19] http://hungarianspectrum.org/2017/09/01/the-orban-governments-penchant-for-religious-educational-institutions/.

curriculum and have far more control over which students they will accept, thus, they can institute very strict disciplinary standards as well as academic standards.

In fact, the government in Hungary plans on spending billions on parochial education over the coming years. For example, they are giving significant grants to the Order of Piarists, which is perhaps the oldest Catholic educational order, for their school system. So, there's no question that Hungary is committed to educating students in Orban's vision for a Christian democracy.

The ramifications for this transference from secular schools to parochial schools for future generations in Hungary really can't be exaggerated. The purpose of secular schools up to this point has not been one of conveying mere religious neutrality, which, of course, is the foundational justification for secularized public schooling. Instead, Orban's government largely recognizes that secularized public schooling is actually about enculturating students in the values of globalism and multiculturalism; Hungarian officials are increasingly aware that secularized schooling is not about religious neutrality; it is about the supremacy of the values of globalism and training students to be disposed towards such values. From what we can gather from the developments in education throughout Hungary, that globalist educational vision is dead. A new vision, one that reveres and protects culture, custom, and tradition rooted in the classical and Christian frames of reference of Western civilization, is rising throughout Hungary, as well as in Poland and increasingly throughout Central Europe, which, in turn, is fostering a European renaissance that promises to transform the lives of students and citizenship for generations to come.

CHAPTER FIVE

Holy Rus': Christian Educational Reforms in Russia

C hristian-based educational developments and reforms are happening throughout the Russian Federation. According to the Home School Legal Defense Association, estimates are that upwards of 100,000 children are currently being homeschooled in Russia, which would make the former Soviet Union second only to the UK in terms of overall European homeschooling numbers.[20] What is certainly helping the homeschool movement is Russia's pro-family education policy; Russian law explicitly states that education is first and foremost the responsibility of the parent. Another factor that's fostering the popularity of homeschooling is its recent endorsement by one of the most famous Russian Orthodox priests, Fr. Dmitry Smirnov. Fr. Dmitry is hugely popular in Russia, he has a widely listened to talk show, where he's a vocal advocate for

---

[20] https://hslda.org/content/hs/international/Russia/201704040.asp.

homeschooling; he has highlighted and interviewed a number of homeschooling organizers and parents on his talk show to help get the word out about the availability of homeschooling and resources for Russian families. We have to remember that 70 percent of Russians identify as Orthodox Christians, and so Fr. Dimitry's endorsement is only fueling the popularity of the practice, as well as underscoring the religious nature of homeschooling. Homeschooling underscores both the primacy of the family in society, as the foundation or basic social unit on the one hand, and the spiritual significance of that foundation on the other.

One of the programs and curriculum that is being translated into Russian is *Classical Conservations*, which is a Christian homeschooling organization that focuses on the classical model of education that was normative; it was, in many respects, the default educational approach in Western civilization for over 2,000 years. Russian conservative Christian activist and homeschooling parent, Alexey Komov is currently overseeing the translation of the *Classical Conservations* curriculum into Russian. And of course, with its Russian Orthodox foundation, classical education is a perfect fit with the renewed vision of Holy Russia that's been fostered since about the year 2000. Scholars have noted that the glue that is holding together post-Soviet Russia is not so much the state, which took a serious beating in terms of trustworthiness in Russia after the collapse of communism. Scholars such as John Burgess have noticed that it is the Orthodox Church which has become the spiritual and ideological glue holding modern Russian society together.[21] The Russian Orthodox Church is basically filling the void left by the collapse of communism, and classical education would simply be an educational extension of this spiritual glue that's reawakening a thoroughly retraditionalized Russian civilization.

In terms of Russian public education, back in 2013, President Putin signed a new law which mandated the study of religion for all Russian students.[22] This measure goes back to 2006, when localities throughout Russia began mandating Russian Orthodox teaching in their public schools, including its traditions, liturgy, and historical figures. The New York Times actually featured a fairly recent article documenting the new curriculum offered in many of Russia's public schools that teaches the basics of the Orthodox faith as part of what Russians are considering to be a truly educated person in the post-Soviet era.[23]

In many respects, these educational reforms are extensions of the Russian notion of *spiritual security*. Spiritual security is considered a subset of national security in a number of policy documents issued by President Putin's administration, which is designed as a primary measure by which traditional Russian values embodied particularly by the Russian Orthodox Church can be protected and perpetuated in the

---

[21] John P. Burgess, *Holy Rus': The Rebirth of Orthodoxy in the New Russia* (New Haven: Yale University Press, 2017).

[22] https://www.christianpost.com/news/russia-makes-religious-education-mandatory-in-schools-87634/.

[23] https://www.nytimes.com/2007/09/23/world/europe/23russia.html.

midst of globalized assaults.[24] It's fully recognized that globalization involves radically detraditionalizing forces that dis-embed time and space away from localized and customary interpretation and control and re-embeds them in transnational consumer-based interpretations. And so, the Russian policy of spiritual security is taking the secular detraditionalizing forces of globalization very seriously. In 2000, the National Security Concept of Russia stated that the assurance of the Russian Federation's national security included protecting the nation's cultural, spiritual, and moral legacy and the historical traditions and standards of public life. There has to be a state policy that maintains the population's spiritual and moral welfare. Vladimir Putin has drawn a very tight connection between religion, culture, and nationality; so much so that back in 2002, the Moscow Patriarch, Alexey II consecrated an Orthodox Church on the grounds of the Lubianka headquarters of the Federal Security Agency, which was formerly known as the KGB. And the key here was the symbolic gesture of bringing together the church and state in maintaining the distinctively Christian identity of Russia. The Russian Patriarch made it very clear that the ceremony solidified the joint effort between departments of the government and the Russian Orthodox Church to maintain the spiritual security of the Russian population.

---

[24] Julie Elkner, "Spiritual Security in Putin's Russia," available at http://historyandpolicy.org/papers/ policy-paper-26.html.

And so, these Christian educational reforms in Russia are yet another indicator that education is indeed going through a process of retraditionalization, which is serving to ensure a far more educated, traditionalist, and indeed conservative future for the Russian Federation.

CHAPTER SIX

The Orthodox Education System in Georgia

F ew nations are exemplifying post-secular trends today than the Republic of Georgia, at the heart of which is the revived Georgian Orthodox Church. What happened is that after the dissolution of the Soviet Union on Christmas of 1991, the Georgian Orthodox Church emerged as the single most trusted, respected, and influential institution in Georgian society. As such, the Georgian Orthodox Church has since filled the mass vacuum that was left with the collapse of communism.

The population of Georgia has consistently been ranked as one of the most religious in the world. Eighty-five percent of the population claims to be Orthodox Christian, with an average weekly church attendance rate of 20 percent, a historic high among European nations.[25] Just to give you an idea of the national commitment to the Georgian Orthodox Church, a recent poll found that 75 percent of respondents said that they would never vote for a political party that was critical of the Georgian Orthodox Church.[26] Needless to say, Georgian politicians are constantly posturing to be seen as pro-Christianity and pro-Orthodox Church; in fact, a politician would have little political legitimacy if they were not in some way endorsed by the Church. In short, after decades of communist rule, the Georgian Orthodox Church has become the symbol of national revival for Georgians.

This cooperation between the church and state has been going on now for some time. Georgia has been a Christian nation since the fourth century when it was the Georgian Kingdom of Kartli. But with the advent of the modern period and ideologically soaked twentieth century, their Christian status was overshadowed for decades under the imprisoning storm clouds of atheistic communism. Once those clouds were lifted, the Church almost instantly became recognized as an indispensable, moral, spiritual, and cultural foundation for the rebuilding of the nation. And so, in the mid-1990s, then-president Eduard Shevardnadze made an informal deal recognizing the public significance of the

---

[25] http://georgiatoday.ge/news/7177/Christianity-in-Georgia%3A-The-Resilience-of-a-Faith-%26-Nation.

[26] https://www.opendemocracy.net/od-russia/eka-chitanava/georgia-s-politics-of-piety.

Church and the benefits bestowed upon it; and since then, the church's influence has only grown in the political arena.

One of the most significant developments that have taken place of late is what's been considered more or less the Christianization of Georgia's public school system, after decades of Soviet-inspired atheism. For nearly two decades now, the Republic of Georgia has been returning to an Eastern Orthodox-based curriculum for their public schools.[27] Interestingly, this re-Christianization of the public school system was actually threatened by the radical secularizing reforms of the government under Mikheil Saakashvili. His attempts to take Eastern Orthodox curriculum and religious symbols out of the public schools elicited a massive backlash, galvanizing the Orthodox Church and groups such as the Orthodox Parents' Union to mobilize a mass blowback against these secularizing efforts. And so, when the elections of 2012 came along, a far more traditionalist party known as the Georgian Dream coalition was elected overwhelmingly, and they immediately reinstituted Eastern Orthodox education into the public schools. The Orthodox Church in this instance became a bulwark defending symbols of Georgian Christian nationalism against globalizing tendencies that sought to re-secularize the nation. In fact, the BBC reported that a 14-year-old boy name Giorgi came home from school all bruised and battered, having obviously suffered physical abuse from his fellow classmates. When asked what instigated the fight, his

---

[27] http://www.bbc.com/news/world-europe-32595514.

parents found out that Giorgi was beaten because he called himself an atheist![28]

Now, while this particular situation is, of course, most unfortunate and hardly one to recommend, it does capture the renewed fervency of the Christian faith in Georgia's public schools. Similar Christianizing processes are going on in Armenia and Moldova as well.[29]

******

What we are seeing in the United States, Hungary, Russia, and Georgia is nothing less than a massive return, a retraditionalizing of their respective educational systems and approaches, which appears to be only the beginning. These educational reforms, blossoming from a revitalized natural family, offer the promise of an exciting future for Christian education, one in which our current renewal is but a mere anticipation. It is my hope that the previous chapters will provide all Christian educators, administrators, and parents the encouragement they need to persevere in the present in light of even better things to come.

---

[28] Ibid.
[29]https://www.academia.edu/17427871/Spiritual_Security_the_Russkiy _Mir_and_the_Russian_Orthodox_Church_The_Influence_of_the_Russi an_Orthodox_Church_on_Russia_s_Foreign_Policy_regarding_Ukraine_ Moldova_Georgia_and_Armenia

Thank you again for purchasing this book!

I hope this book gave you the encouragement you need to know that what we are doing in Christian education is only the beginning; we are in store for even more amazing things yet to come.

If you enjoyed this book, then I'd like to ask you for a favor: Would you be kind enough to leave a review for this book on Amazon? I would so greatly appreciate it!

Thank you so much, and may God richly bless you!

Steve Turley

www.turleytalks.com

Check Out My Other Books

Below you'll find some of my other popular books that are popular on Amazon. Simply go to the links below to check them out. Alternatively, you can visit my author page on Amazon to see my other works.

- *Uprising: How the Yellow Vest Protests are Changing France and Overturning the World Order* https://amzn.to/2EqwTRn

- *The Abolition of Sanity: C.S. Lewis on the Consequences of Modernism* https://amzn.to/2IAlGkg

- *The Return of Christendom: Demography, Politics, and the Coming Christian Majority* https://amzn.to/2VM2W4O

- *The New Nationalism: How the Populist Right is Defeating Globalism and Awakening a New Political Order* https://amzn.to/2WEP11u

- *The Triumph of Tradition: How the Resurgence of Religion is Reawakening a Conservative World* https://amzn.to/2xieNO3

- *Classical vs. Modern Education: A Vision from C.S. Lewis* http://amzn.to/2opDZju

- *President Trump and Our Post-Secular Future: How the 2016 Election Signals the Dawning of a Conservative Nationalist Age* http://amzn.to/2B87Q22

- *Gazing: Encountering the Mystery of Art* https://amzn.to/2yKi6k9

- *Beauty Matters: Creating a High Aesthetic in School Culture* https://amzn.to/2L8Ejd7

- *Ever After: How to Overcome Cynical Students with the Role of Wonder in Education* http://amzn.to/2jbJI78

- *Movies and the Moral Imagination: Finding Paradise in Films* http://amzn.to/2zjghJj

- *Echoes of Eternity: A Classical Guide to Music* https://amzn.to/2O0bYrY

- *Health Care Sharing Ministries: How Christians are Revolutionizing Medical Cost and Care* http://amzn.to/2B2Q8B2

- *The Face of Infinite of Love: Athanasius on the Incarnation* http://amzn.to/2oxULNM

- *Stressed Out: Learn How an Ancient Christian Practice Can Relieve Stress and Overcome Anxiety* http://amzn.to/2kFzcpc

- *Wise Choice: Six Steps to Godly Decision Making* http://amzn.to/2qy3C2Z

- *Awakening Wonder: A Classical Guide to Truth, Goodness, and Beauty* http://amzn.to/2ziKR5H

- *Worldview Guide for* A Christmas Carol http://amzn.to/2BCcKHO

- *The Ritualized Revelation of the Messianic Age: Washings and Meals in Galatians and 1 Corinthians* http://amzn.to/2B0mGvf

If the links do not work, for whatever reason, you can simply search for these titles on the Amazon website to find them.

About www.TurleyTalks.com

Are we seeing the revitalization of Christian civilization?

For decades, the world has been dominated by a process known as globalization, an economic and political system that hollows out and erodes a culture's traditions, customs, and religions, all the while conditioning populations to rely on the expertise of a tiny class of technocrats for every aspect of their social and economic lives.

Until now.

All over the world, there's been a massive blowback against the anti-cultural processes of globalization and its secular aristocracy. From Russia to Europe and now in the U.S., citizens are rising up and reasserting their religion, culture, and nation as mechanisms of resistance against the dehumanizing tendencies of secularism and globalism.

And it's just the beginning.

The secular world is at its brink, and a new traditionalist age is rising.

Join me each week as we examine these worldwide trends, discover answers to today's toughest challenges, and together learn to live in the present in light of even better things to come.

So hop on over to www.TurleyTalks.com and have a look around. Make sure to sign-up for our weekly Email Newsletter where you'll get lots of free giveaways, private Q&As, and tons of great content. Check out our YouTube channel (www.youtube.com/c/DrSteveTurley) where you'll understand current events in light of conservative trends to help you flourish in your personal and professional life. And of course, 'Like' us on Facebook and follow us on Twitter.

Thank you so much for your support and for your part in this cultural renewal.

About the Author

Steve Turley (PhD, Durham University) is an internationally recognized scholar, speaker, and classical guitarist. He is the author of over a dozen books, including *Classical vs. Modern Education: A Vision from C.S. Lewis, Awakening Wonder: A Classical Guide to Truth, Goodness, and Beauty*, and *The Ritualized Revelation of the Messianic Age: Washings and Meals in Galatians and 1 Corinthians*. Steve's popular YouTube channel showcases weekly his expertise in the rise of nationalism, populism, and traditionalism throughout the world, and his podcasts and writings on civilization, society, culture, education, and the arts are widely accessed at TurleyTalks.com. He is a faculty member at Tall Oaks Classical School in Bear, DE, where he teaches Theology and Rhetoric, and was formerly Professor of Fine Arts at Eastern University. Steve lectures at universities, conferences, and churches throughout the U.S. and abroad. His research and writings have appeared in such journals as *Christianity and Literature, Calvin Theological Journal, First Things, Touchstone*, and *The*

Chesterton Review. He and his wife, Akiko, have four children and live in Newark, DE, where they together enjoy fishing, gardening, and watching *Duck Dynasty* marathons.

Made in the USA
Lexington, KY
11 December 2019